Anglican – Orthodox Dialogue

The Dublin Agreed Statement 1984

ST. VLADIMIR'S SEMINARY PRESS
Crestwood, New York 10707
1985

First published in the USA 1985
St. Vladimir's Seminary Press,
575 Scarsdale Road, Crestwood, NY 10707

Parallel edition published in Great Britain 1985 by SPCK

ISBN 0-88141-047-0

Library of Congress Cataloging in Publication Data
Main entry under title:

Anglican–Orthodox dialogue.

    Based on discussions held at the 1984 meeting
of the Anglican–Orthodox Joint Doctrinal
Commission at Bellinter near Dublin.
    Includes bibliographies.
    1. Anglican Communion—Relations—Orthodox
Eastern Church—Congresses.   2. Orthodox
Eastern Church—Relations—Anglican Communion—
Congresses.   3. Christian Union—Congresses.
I. Anglican–Orthodox Joint Doctrinal Commission.
BX5004.3.A5   1984   272'.72   85-1766
ISBN 0-88141-047-0

Typeset by Academic Typing & Typesetting Service,
Gerrards Cross, Buckinghamshire, England
Printed in Great Britain by
Hollen Street Press Ltd, Slough, Berks

CONTENTS

ABBREVIATIONS

ACC	Anglican Consultative Council
AOJDD	Anglican–Orthodox Joint Doctrinal Discussions
ARCIC	Anglican–Roman Catholic International Commission
ECNL	Eastern Churches Newsletter
PG	Migne, J.-P., *Patrologia Graeca*
PL	Migne, J.-P., *Patrologia Latina*

PREFACE

It was Archbishop Basil of Brussels, one of the most revered Orthodox members of the Anglican–Orthodox Joint Doctrinal Commission, who remarked that the aim of our Dialogue is that we may eventually be visibly united in one Church. We offer this Report in the conviction that although this goal may presently seem to be far from being achieved, it is nevertheless one towards which God the Holy Spirit is insistently beckoning us. Those who have served on the Commission at every stage since its inception in 1966, and since our own Co-Chairmenship began in 1980, have been aware that this is the case, although we may sometimes have been tempted to think otherwise. Not only is there a long-standing friendship between the Anglican Communion and the Orthodox Churches but we have not been allowed to forget that the continuation of such friendship is both costly and demanding.

As those who read this document will see, we have been studying for eight years some of the basic aspects of our Holy Faith. As bishops, clergy and lay theologians representing our Churches in many parts of the world we have not hesitated to voice our differences as well as our agreements. There are still more to be faced. Yet, as we debate together, and above all as we celebrate the Holy Liturgy and other services daily during the week-long meetings according to the Rites of our Churches, we are convinced that we are being slowly but surely moulded by the Spirit into the patterns of love and understanding which, when God knows we are ready for it, will eventually lead to visible unity.

Such experiences do not achieve their true end unless they are shared with the bishops, clergy and faithful people of our respective Churches. We hope that this new Agreed Statement completed in Dublin will provide a fresh opportunity for many Anglicans and Orthodox to study our faith together. For while we press on in the work of our Commission we are equally anxious to do all we can to encourage visits among the bishops of our Churches; and also the participation of synodical, diocesan and parish gatherings, wherever our Churches live side by side, in the exciting tasks of rediscovering one another in Christ; of sharing in the richness of each other's traditions; and, as we recognize the poverty caused by our long separations, together serving others in the Name of the One who prayed to his Father:

> I do not pray for these only, but also for those who believe in me through their word, that they may all be one; even as thou, Father, art in me, and I in thee, that they also may be in us, so that the world may believe that thou hast sent me. (John 17.20–1).

CO-CHAIRMEN

†Henry Hill   †Methodios of Thyateira and Great Britain

Dublin, 19 August 1984

INTRODUCTION
ANGLICAN–ORTHODOX DIALOGUE 1976–84

1   Background

As a result of the talks in 1962 between the Archbishop of Canterbury, Dr Michael Ramsey, and the Ecumenical Patriarch, Athenagoras I of Constantinople, the Primates of the Anglican Communion were approached and agreed unanimously to the setting up of an Anglican Theological Commission to confer with theologians of the Orthodox Churches. In 1964 the Third Pan–Orthodox Conference at Rhodes unanimously decided officially to resume dialogue with the Anglican Communion, and this was ratified by all the Orthodox Churches. After a preparatory phase (1966–72) in which the Anglican and Orthodox Commissions met separately, the first series of joint conversations took place (1973–6) and resulted in the production of the Moscow Agreed Statement on the Knowledge of God, the Inspiration and Authority of Holy Scripture, Scripture and Tradition, the Authority of the Councils, the *Filioque* Clause, the Church as the Eucharistic Community, and the Invocation of the Holy Spirit in the Eucharist.[1]

2   From Moscow to Lambeth (1976–8)

The Ecumenical Patriarch Athenagoras I described Archbishop Michael Ramsey's 1962 visit to Constantinople as 'the beginning of a new spiritual spring that may lead to greater rapprochement and the closer collaboration of all churches'.[2] During his visit to the Ecumenical Patriarch Demetrios I in 1982 Archbishop Robert Runcie of Canterbury referred to that earlier remark and then spoke of the first series of Anglican–

Orthodox conversations as a 'spiritual summer' with the Moscow Agreed Statement as its 'first-fruits'. He next went on to speak of a 'wintry season' of difficulties experienced in Anglican–Orthodox relations.[3] For when the Anglican–Orthodox Joint Doctrinal Commission met at Cambridge in 1977 to study the subjects agreed at the conclusion of the Moscow Conference (1. The Church and the Churches; 2. The Communion of Saints and the departed; 3. Ministry and priesthood),[4] a 'thunderstorm' broke out presaging the onset of 'winter'. For the Orthodox members 'realised with regret' that the ordination of women was 'no longer simply a question for discussion but an actual event in the life of some of the Anglican churches' and asked themselves 'how it will be possible to continue the dialogue, and what meaning the dialogue will have in these circumstances'.[5] It was therefore agreed that the 1978 meeting would take place 'before the Lambeth Conference, in order, by expounding the Orthodox position, to enable their Anglican brethren to come to what, in their view, would be a proper appreciation of the matter. For the Orthodox the future of the Dialogue would depend on the resolutions of the Lambeth Conference.'[6] In February 1978 the Bishop of St Albans told the General Synod of the Church of England that 'the future as well as the character of these valuable doctrinal discussions now hangs in the balance'.

The main part of the 1978 Conference at Moni Pendeli, Athens, was devoted to setting out the Orthodox and Anglican positions on the Ordination of Women to the Priesthood. In its report the Orthodox members said: 'We see the ordination of women, not as part of the creative continuity of tradition, but as a violation of the apostolic faith and order of the Church . . . This will have a decisively negative effect on the issue of the recognition of Anglican orders . . . By ordaining women

Anglicans would sever themselves from continuity in apostolic faith and spiritual life.' They added: 'It is obvious that, if the dialogue continues, its character would be drastically changed.' The joint conclusions to the report stated: 'We value our Dialogue together and we are encouraged that our Churches and their leaders, as well as the members of our Commission, hope that it may continue under conditions acceptable to both sides.'[7]

Following the 1978 Lambeth Conference's Resolution 21 on the ordination of women,[8] the Orthodox Co-Chairman of AOJDD, Archbishop Athenagoras, expressed his view that 'the theological dialogue will continue, although now simply as an academic and informative exercise, and no longer as an ecclesial endeavour aiming at the union of the two churches'. He later recommended that Orthodox professors rather than bishops should take part in the dialogue as an indication of its changed status and purpose. Some Orthodox agreed with this. However, as the Bishop of St Albans discovered during his visits to the Orthodox Churches in the spring of 1979, other Orthodox felt there was no need to change the standing of the talks and wished the dialogue to be resumed in order, as the Lambeth Conference 1978 Resolution 35:2 put it, 'to explore the fundamental questions of doctrinal agreement and disagreement in our Churches'.[9] This view prevailed, and in July 1979 the Steering Committee of AOJDD met and agreed that the Full Commission should continue its work in July 1980. 'The ultimate aim remains the unity of the Churches', it affirmed. But 'the method may need to change in order to emphasise the pastoral and practical dimensions of the subjects of theological discussions'. It concluded: 'Our conversations are concerned with the search for a unity in faith. They are not negotiations for immediate full communion. When this is understood the discovery of differences on various matters, though distressing, will be seen as a necessary step on the long road toward that unity which God wills for His Church.'

3. From Llandaff to Dublin (1980–4)

During his visit to the Ecumenical Patriarch of Constantinople in 1982, the Archbishop of Canterbury, Dr Robert Runcie, 'spoke with gratitude of His All-Holiness' encouragement to continue the dialogue particularly when facing difficulties, which had led to the "second spring" which these official conversations were now experiencing'.[10] The Commission resumed its work at St Michael's College, Llandaff, in July 1980, and welcomed as its new Co-Chairmen Bishop Henry Hill of Ontario, Canada (following the appointment of the Bishop of St Albans as Archbishop of Canterbury) and Archbishop Methodios of Thyateira and Great Britain (following the death of his predecessor Archbishop Athenagoras). The Commission approved a report on 'The Communion of Saints and the Departed', and continued work on 'The Church and the Churches' and on the *Filioque* clause in the Creed. This was continued and extended at subsequent meetings at the Orthodox Patriarchal Centre at Chambésy in Geneva 1981, and at Canterbury in 1982 where the first sub-commission focused on 'The Mystery of the Church', the second sub-commission on 'Participation in the Grace of the Holy Trinity and Christian Holiness', and the third sub-commission on 'Tradition, Christian Worship, and the Maintenance of the Christian Faith'. At the Commission's meeting at Odessa in the Soviet Union in 1983, particular attention was given to new material on Primacy (Seniority); Witness, Evangelism, and Service; and on Prayer, Icons, and Family Devotion, and discussion of the topics already on the agenda was continued. The 1984 meeting at Bellinter near Dublin has had the task of finalizing an agreed Report and Statement on 'The Mystery of the Church', 'Faith in the Trinity, Prayer and Holiness', and on 'Worship and Tradition'.

4 Conclusion

After the difficulties of the fairly recent past, the Anglican–Orthodox Joint Doctrinal Commission has re-established itself and has now developed a productive and satisfactory way of working. There is a freshness and liveliness brought into the Commission by the presence of so many new members both Anglican and Orthodox, as well as much valued continuity and a wealth of experience provided by its older and longer-serving members. There is a prayerfulness which permeates its whole work, and which has brought the Commission to a new stage of fellowship in Christ. Also, some of the pressures of the past have gone. We are not required to solve outstanding problems (such as the ordination of women) as a condition of continuing the dialogue. Nor are we trying to produce too quickly materials that might be used as the basis for early decisions to enter a new stage of relationships between our Churches. Instead, the Commission is more free to explore together and understand better the faith we hold and the ways in which we express it. It is also note-worthy that far more consideration has been given to prayer and spirituality than is usual in inter-church encounters of this type. If we accept that Anglican–Orthodox Dialogue is still in the *first* stage of exploring each other's faith and seeking co-operation in mission and service,[11] then it can perhaps be seen that much good work is being done by this particular bilateral conversation to help bridge the ancient divide between Eastern and Western Churches.

During the Archbishop of Canterbury's visit to Constantinople in 1982, Archbishop Methodios of Thyateira and Great Britain, the Orthodox Co-Chairman of the Joint Doctrinal Commission, said: 'There is positive progress towards the first stage of common prayer and co-operation.'

Members of the Commission are convinced, as an Anglican Consultative Council report has said, that their work contributes greatly to 'the mission and peace of the Churches after the ancient division of East and West', and to the Church's ministry of reconciliation and peace 'in the midst of world political tensions and their resulting pressures'.[12]

International Anglican–Orthodox Dialogue both draws from and seeks to promote local Anglican–Orthodox dialogue, remembering that the latter's task is not to duplicate but to make known International Agreements and to develop relationships between the people of the two Churches.

Anglican–Orthodox discussions take place in the context of Anglican–Roman Catholic, Orthodox–Roman Catholic and other bilateral and multilateral conversations. Each draws from and contributes to the other. We are convinced that our discussions have a further part to play in East-West relations, in inter-church relations and in theological explorations from which we all benefit.

NOTES

1   Published with introductory and supporting material in *Anglican–Orthodox Dialogue: The Moscow Agreed Statement*, ed. K. Ware and C. Davey (SPCK 1977), reproduced in Appendix I below.

2   Colin Davey, 'Anglican–Orthodox Relations during the Patriarchate of His All-Holiness Athenagoras I (1948–72)' in *Athenagoras, the Epirote Ecumenical Patriarch* (Ioannina 1976), p. 417.

3   Communiqué 1 August 1982 para. 4. *Episkepsis* No. 278 (1.9.1982), p. 2.

4   *Anglican-Orthodox Dialogue*, p. 78.

5   Communiqué from Cambridge Conference.

6   ibid.

7   Report of the Athens meeting paras. III 4, 5, 6; V.

8   *The Report of the Lambeth Conference 1978*, pp. 45-7.

9   ibid., p. 51.

10   Communiqué para. 4. *Episkepsis* No. 278 (1.9.1982), p. 2.

11   See Anglican Consultative Council 1982 Consultation: Unity by Stages, Section III (a).

12   *Steps towards Unity*, Report of the ACC Preparatory Group on Ecumenical Affairs, Woking, February 1984, p. 14.

The Agreed Statement

Method and Approach

1   In our discussions since the adoption of the Moscow Agreed Statement, and especially during the last four years, our Joint Commission has endeavoured to keep constantly in mind the essential link that exists between theology and sanctification through prayer, between doctrine and the daily life of the Christian community. Keenly aware how dangerous it is to discuss the Christian faith in an abstract manner, we have sought always to understand how theological principles are expressed in the living experience of the people of God.

I THE MYSTERY OF THE CHURCH

Approaches to the Mystery

2 We live in a deeply divided world. We are aware that Christian disunity, as well as being contrary to the will of God and a sin against the very nature of the Church, has often contributed towards the divisions of the world. We know that the Church is entrusted with a message of reconciliation. This drives us to seek unity amongst ourselves, in order to contribute to the healing of the divisions of humankind, as well as to stand together as Christians who face difficulties and pressures, and who witness to Christ's truth in a hostile or indifferent world. We know the temptation for Christian communities to avoid this challenge. But Christ has poured out his Spirit on his people, to transform them 'into his likeness from one degree of glory to another' (2 Cor. 3.18), and to incorporate them in his mission of love and reconciliation to the world (2 Cor. 5.18; John 20.21).

3. The mystery of the Church cannot be defined or fully described. But the steadfast joy of people who discover new life and salvation in Christ through the Church reminds us that the Church itself is a lived experience. The Church is sent into the world as a sign, instrument and first-fruits of the Kingdom of God. The New Testament speaks about it primarily in images, such as the following:

4 (a) The Church is 'the body of Christ' (1 Cor. 12.27). The head is Christ (Eph. 1.22; Col. 1.18), and his members are those who in faith respond to the gospel (Rom. 10.17), are baptized in the name of the Father, the Son, and the Holy Spirit (Matt. 28.19), and are

united with Christ and with each other through participation in the Eucharist (1 Cor. 10.16–17). Through this union they are being conformed to his true humanity, filled with his divinity, and made 'partakers of the divine nature' (2 Pet. 1.4) ($\theta\acute{\epsilon}\omega\sigma\iota\varsigma$). In its totality the Church incorporates both living and departed in the communion of the saints.

5   (*b*) The Church is the messianic gathering, the gathering in Christ of all nations into the people of God (Matt. 8.11; Gal. 3.8), and, as the new Israel, completes the special sign of God's grace given in the election of the ancient people of Israel as God's chosen and beloved (Gal. 3.8; Rev. 21.2–3).

6   (*c*) The Church is the holy temple of God, indwelt by his Spirit (1 Cor. 3.16; Eph. 2.22). It is a spiritual house, a royal priesthood appointed to declare to the world the wonderful deeds of him who called them out of darkness into light (1 Pet. 2.5–9).

7   (*d*) The New Testament also speaks of the Church as Christ's bride, whom he presents to himself 'without spot or wrinkle or any such thing' (Eph. 5.27; cf. 2 Cor. 11.2). In this connection Scripture looks forward to the consummation of history as 'the marriage of the Lamb', when the bride will be prepared to meet her bridegroom in glory (Rev. 19.6–8).

The Marks of the Church

8   In the Creed we proclaim the Church to be one, holy, catholic and apostolic.

(*a*) The Church is one, because there is a 'one Lord, one faith, one baptism, one God and Father of us all' (Eph. 4.5), and it participates in the life of the Holy Trinity, one God in three persons. The unity of the

Church is expressed in common faith and in the fellowship of the Holy Spirit; it takes concrete and visible form as the Church, gathered round the bishop in the common celebration of the Holy Eucharist, proclaims Christ's death till he comes (1 Cor. 11.26). The unity of Christians with Christ in baptism is a unity of love and mutual respect which transcends all human division, of race, social status and sex (Gal. 3.28). This unity in Christ is God's gift to the world by which men and women may learn to live in unity with one another, accepting one another as Christ has accepted them.

9 Nevertheless, we find ourselves in an abnormal situation. We are a disrupted Christian people seeking to restore our unity. Our divisions do not destroy but they damage the basic unity we have in Christ, and our disunity impedes our mission to the world as well as our relationships with each other. Anglicans are accustomed to seeing our divisions as within the Church: they do not believe that they alone are the one true Church, but they believe that they belong to it. Orthodox, however, believe that the Orthodox Church is the one true Church of Christ, which as his Body is not and cannot be divided. But at the same time they see Anglicans as brothers and sisters in Christ who are seeking with them the union of all Christians in the one Church.

10 (b) The Church is holy (1 Cor. 3.17) because its members are in Christ, the head, who is holy and who lives in them (Eph. 3.17). The Church's holiness can be obscured but cannot be destroyed by the sins of its members. Christ's holiness is shown, not in drawing apart from outcasts and sinners but in calling them (Mark 2.15–17), and most fully in his becoming sin for us in order to deliver us from sin (2 Cor. 5.21). For through his life, death and resurrection he overcomes, redeems and sanctifies the world, and by his justifying

grace transforms forgiven sinners into 'a holy people' (1 Pet. 2.9). The Church's holiness springs from the action of God's Holy Spirit whom Christ sends to purify his people, to draw them into the reality of his risen life, and to conform them to his compassion and love for the world.

11　The pursuit of holiness challenges the world and may bring Christians into conflict with it, as they carry on Christ's spiritual warfare with the powers of evil. In this they are following the saints of the Church who have shared in Christ's rejection and sufferings (Col. 1.24), 'in honour and dishonour, in ill repute and good repute' (2 Cor. 6.8).

12　(*c*) The Church is catholic because by word and life it maintains and bears witness to the fullness of the faith, and because people of all nations and conditions are called to participate in it. Catholicity stands in contrast to schism and heresy. If Christians cease to love each other or to respect church order they are in danger of schism. If they depart from the essentials of the apostolic faith they become guilty of heresy. The catholicity of the Church is shown in the multiplicity of particular local churches, each of which, being in eucharistic communion with all the other local churches, manifests in its own place and time the one catholic Church. These local churches, in faithful response to their own particular missionary situation, have developed a wide diversity in their life. As long as their witness to the one faith remains unimpaired, such diversity is to be seen, not as a deficiency or cause for division, but as a mark of the fullness of the one Spirit who distributes to each according to his will (1 Cor. 12.11).

13　At each local Eucharist, celebrated within the catholic Church, Christ is present in his wholeness, and so each local celebration actualizes and gives visible expression to the Church's catholicity.[1] Communion in the Eucharist is also the outward manifestation of the common faith and the Christian love which binds together all the local churches in the one catholic Church. Their communion is likewise expressed in the constant contact and communication between the bishops and members of different local churches through meetings in council, exchange of letters, mutual visits, and prayer for each other.

14   (*d*) The Church is apostolic because it is built on the foundation of the apostles (Eph. 2.20; Rev. 21.14) who are the primary and authoritative witnesses to the crucified and risen Lord. Their authority lies in the fact that they were sent by Jesus Christ, who was himself sent by the Father (Matt. 28.19–20; John 20.21). Christ gave them the Holy Spirit, who maintains the apostolic word as a living force within the Church, evoking faith and discipleship. The Church's apostolicity is manifested chiefly in three ways:

15   (*i*) The Church maintains the apostolic tradition by its preaching and teaching and by a constantly renewed understanding and living of Scripture. By critical discernment it rejects inauthentic ways of thought and life.[2]

16   (*ii*) The Church in each generation participates in the apostolic mission to the world. The Church is 'not of the world' (John 17.14), but it is in, with and for human society. Its mission is to save and transform society by the power of the Holy Spirit. This mission includes preaching, teaching, worship, diakonia, testimony against injustice; also the hidden life of prayer, and martyrdom.

17   (*iii*) The apostolicity of the Church is manifested

in a particular way through the succession of bishops. This succession is a sign of the unbroken continuity of apostolic tradition and life. Through prayer and the laying on of hands, the bishop receives the Holy Spirit, who bestows on him a *charisma* giving him the grace and responsibility to uphold and testify to the authority of the apostolic word (2 Tim. 1.6). The local bishop can only perform his ministry: (1) in unity with his brother bishops, especially when meeting synodically; (2) in unity with his flock, both clergy and laity. In exercising the ministry of oversight he should pay heed to the prophetic and other gifts which Christ gives his people (Rom. 12.6–8; Eph. 4.11–12).

Communion and Intercommunion

18   (*a*) The several Provinces of the Anglican Communion have their own synodical regulations governing eucharistic hospitality and relationships of reciprocal intercommunion and Full Communion with other churches. There are some instances where the pastoral concern for individuals is uppermost. There are others where there have been specific joint Declarations of Intent to work together locally or nationally to seek unity (such as that between members of Local Ecumenical Projects in England or between Anglicans, Methodists, Presbyterians, and Congregationalists in South Africa). There are still others where unity of faith, ministry and sacraments is accompanied by growth in conciliarity and common mission. From all of these it is clear that there has been a considerable development in ecumenical and inter-church relations in recent years, which has resulted in Anglicans sharing in the Eucharist with members of other churches on special ecumenical occasions, in times of special need, or on a more regular basis.

19   Anglicans have come to recognize different stages in which churches stand in a progressively closer relationship to each other, with a corresponding and consequent degree of eucharistic sharing which is viewed as both 'a proper manifestation of such unity in Christ as they already share' and as 'creative of even greater unity'.[3] However, 'for a Church officially to authorise Intercommunion (whether "Reciprocal" or "Limited") as a *means* to unity, or for an individual to practise it, where there is already some agreement in faith and commitment to unity, is not to deny that a more complete expression, such as Full Communion or Organic Union, is also a goal to be sought'.[4]

20   (*b*) For the Orthodox, 'communion' involves a mystical and sanctifying unity created by the Body and Blood of Christ, which makes them 'one body and one blood (σύσσωμοι καὶ σύναιμοι) with Christ',[5] and therefore they can have no differences of faith. There can be 'communion' only between local churches which have a unity of faith, ministry, and sacraments. For this reason the concept of 'Intercommunion' has no place in Orthodox ecclesiology.

Wider Leadership within the Church

21   (*a*) Throughout the history of the Church, from the New Testament onwards, there can be seen varying patterns of wider leadership. Anglicans often refer to these as levels of 'primacy', whereas Orthodox generally prefer to speak about an order of 'seniority' (πρεσβεία). Despite differences in the outward forms in which this wider leadership is expressed, there is fundamental agreement between the way in which Anglicans understand 'primacy' and the way in which Orthodox understand 'seniority'.

22   (*b*) In the New Testament there are certain persons within the Church who are vested with special authority, such as Peter, Paul, James and John, but none of these acts in isolation. The entire New Testament points to the independence or autonomy of local churches, which live together in unity, yet with no single church possessing permanent pre-eminence. Following the adoption of Christianity as the official religion of the Roman Empire, an order of seniority became established, involving five great sees in the following sequence: Rome, Constantinople, Alexandria, Antioch, Jerusalem (see the canons of the Ecumenical Councils, especially Canon 2 of Constantinople [381] and Canon 28 of Chalcedon [451]). Both the apostolic foundation of sees and the civil status of cities as centres of communication influenced the development of this order of seniority.

23   (*c*) This wider leadership, whether described as 'seniority' or 'primacy', is to be understood in terms not of coercion but of pastoral service. Jesus warned his apostles, both by word and by example, to exercise their authority not by lording it over the flock but by being servants of all (Mark 10.42–5; John 13.12–17); and the same warning was repeated to those who succeeded the apostles in the oversight of the Church (1 Pet. 5.1–4). Since in practice this teaching has often been forgotten, it is good that the Anglican–Roman Catholic International Commission has called attention to it, noting that 'truly to lead is to serve and not to dominate others', and that the bishop has his authority in order to serve his flock as its shepherd'.[6] This is to be kept in mind whenever the word 'honour' is applied to a bishop, as in the phrase 'seniority of honour' (πρεσβεία τῆς τιμῆς).

24   (*d*) Wider leadership exists at various levels:

(*i*) There is first the seniority of the bishop who presides over a group of diocesan bishops. Such seniority is held in modern Orthodox practice by the patriarch within each patriarchate, or by the presiding archbishop or metropolitan within each autocephalous or autonomous Church; in Anglican practice, by the archbishop or presiding bishop within each province of the Anglican Communion.

(*ii*) Secondly, there exist various different forms of seniority on the universal level, such as that of the Pope within the Roman Catholic Church (and throughout the whole Christian Church prior to the schism); that of the Ecumenical Patriarch within the Orthodox Church; and that of the Archbishop of Canterbury within the worldwide Anglican Communion.

25 (*e*) It is the purpose of wider leadership to strengthen unity and to give brotherly help to the bishops of the local churches in the exercise of their common ministry which exists to safeguard scriptural truth whenever it is threatened, to promote right teaching and living, and to further the Church's mission to the world. This the bishop who has seniority does chiefly in two ways:

(*i*) He encourages Christian fellowship and collaboration by initiating procedures which will lead to the summoning of a council or synod, and presiding over it.

(*ii*) In certain situations, when appeals are made to him from the decisions of a diocesan bishop or a group of bishops, he initiates procedures whereby these decisions may be reviewed.

But the bishop who has seniority does not have the right to intervene arbitrarily in the affairs of a diocese other than his own.[7]

26 (*f*) In exercising his ministry the bishop who has seniority should respect the proper authority and freedom of each diocese or local church. He should always act in collegiality with his brother bishops; equally he should take account of the gifts of understanding and discernment entrusted to the whole people of God, clergy and laity together.

27 (*g*) The Ecumenical Councils ascribe a position of special seniority, within the wider leadership of the universal Church, not only to the See of Rome but also to that of Constantinople; and this fact needs to be taken into account in any Christian reunion.[8] The ecumenical Patriarch does not, however, claim universal jurisdiction over the other Churches, such as is ascribed to the Pope by the First and also the Second Vatican Council; and Orthodox see any such claim as contrary to the meaning of seniority, as this was understood in the early centuries of the Church.

28 The Anglican Churches of the British Isles, since their separation from the See of Rome, have developed into an international communion; and within this communion a position of seniority has come to be ascribed to the ancient See of Canterbury. But this seniority is understood as a ministry of service and support to the other Anglican Churches, not as a form of domination over them; and, like the Ecumenical Patriarch, the Archbishop of Canterbury makes no claim to a primacy of universal jurisdiction. Thus, even though the seniority ascribed to the Archbishop of Canterbury is not identical with that given to the Ecumenical Patriarch, the Anglican Communion has developed on the Orthodox rather than the Roman Catholic pattern, as a fellowship of self-governing national or regional Churches.

29 (*h*) According to Roman Catholic teaching the

primacy of the Pope is closely linked to his infallibility. Both Orthodox and Anglicans consider that infallibility is not the property of any particular person within the Church.[9] It is significant that the Anglican–Roman Catholic International Commission has stated clearly: 'This is a term applicable unconditionally only to God, and . . . to use it of a human being, even in highly restricted circumstances, can produce many misunderstandings'.[10]

30   Anglicans and Orthodox are both firmly convinced that the Holy Spirit will guide the Church into all truth and 'the powers of death shall not prevail against it' (Matt. 16.18). We believe that all bishops are empowered by the Holy Spirit to bear witness to the truth; but if the doctrine of infallibility means that it is possible to guarantee by external criteria that certain statements of a particular bishop are safeguarded from error, we cannot accept this. Equally no such guarantee can be given concerning the statements of an episcopal assembly, since the ecumenicity of a council is manifested through its acceptance by the body of the Church.

Witness, Evangelism and Service

31   God bears witness to himself by his revelation in creation (Rom. 1.19–20; Acts 14.17), through the patriarchs and prophets and finally through his Son Jesus Christ (Heb. 1.1–2), who is 'the faithful and true witness' (Rev. 3.14). Christ is also the true Servant, who turned upside down our ideas of leadership by becoming 'the servant of all'[11] and by serving mankind in his obedient and sacrificial ministry, suffering and death. God's revelation of himself in Christ necessarily involved conflict with evil, which brought him to the cross. So God's highest service to mankind – the bringing

of salvation in Christ – is at the same time his profound-est witness to himself in and through Christ's sacrifice on the cross. Christ is witness (μάρτυς) as well as teacher, healer and saviour. The primary movement of witness and service is therefore from God to the world, and it includes his affirmation of the sanctity of life, his testimony against all that is evil, and also his call to all mankind to 'repent, and believe in the gospel' (Mark 1.15).

32   This movement is continued in the Church, the Body of Christ, when in the power of the Holy Spirit it responds to God's call and offers itself in witness and service to the world. The Church's witness and evangel-ism call men to hear the good news and to receive the saving grace of Christ. The apostolic Church exists by mission as fire exists by burning. Mission is not merely one of many items of business for the Church or for a department of the Church. The members of the Church are to be judged not least by what they do to reach unbelievers. The evangelizing of one person by another is the responsibility of lay people and clergy alike. The Church's mission also includes its service of mankind, which brings the healing, forgiveness, love and compas-sion of Christ to people in need, people in conflict and people in the grip of sin and evil.

33   Witness, evangelism, service, worship and sacrifice belong together, for these are different sides of the same reality. So testimony in the name of Jesus rightly given is also a service to one's neighbour; ministry rightly per-formed in the name of Christ constitutes a witness to Jesus. Worship (λειτουργία) involves service of the people (its ancient meaning), when we worship Christ by ministering to him in the sick, the prisoner and the needy (Matt. 25.37–40). Where the Church is not at liberty to organize developed social and philanthropic

programmes of its own or to take part in those organized jointly with others, its witness is carried out through worship, prayer and personal ministry. The Church can bear witness not only in word and deed but also in silence. Lives dedicated to service proclaim the gospel. Sacrificial self-giving, suffering and death may result from testimony to the truth of the gospel – or from testimony against injustice, which is also testimony to the truth of God's concern for the poor and the oppressed.

34   Evangelism involves the Church in social action which can be an authentic witness to the gospel and should not be separated from it or contrasted with it. The Church should not engage in a social programme that becomes an end in itself, for 'man shall not live by bread alone, but by every word that proceeds from the mouth of God' (Matt. 4.4). The spirit in which Christians act is different from that of humanism or secularism. It is informed by a sense of God's grace, of sin and the need for repentance and by an eschatological perspective. Nevertheless Christians are right to be involved in the life of the world and in the wider struggle for justice, freedom and peace, and for the removal of everything which threatens the sacred gift of life to all mankind.

35   The Church's witness and service minister to people's deepest spiritual, physical and social needs. But in carrying out this mission the Church's stance should be one of continual vigilance, as it lives 'in the world', but is 'not of the world' (John 17.11–16) and as it seeks to be faithful to Christ the true witness and servant.

NOTES

1   See the Moscow Agreed Statement Section VI, 'The Church as the Eucharistic Community'.

2   See the Moscow Agreed Statement Section III, 'Scripture and Tradition'.

3   *Intercommunion: A Scottish Episcopalian Approach* (1969), p. 10.

4   ACC Study paper on 'Full Communion' (1981), p. 7.

5   *PG* 33, 1100 A7, or *PG* 96, 1409 D8, 9.

6   Authority in the Church II, 5 and 17, in *The Final Report* of ARCIC, pp. 83 and 89.

7   The statement in Authority in the Church II, 20 (ibid. p. 90) requires further elucidation.

8   In this connection we would wish to qualify what is said in the ARCIC report Authority in the Church I, 23 (ibid. p. 64).

9   See the Moscow Agreed Statement IV para. 17–18.

10 Authority in the Church II, 32 (op. cit. p. 97).

11 Polycarp, *Letter to the Philippians*, 5:2; cf. Mark 10.45.

II FAITH IN THE TRINITY, PRAYER AND HOLINESS

Participation in the grace of the Holy Trinity

36 Trinitarian doctrine presupposes participation in the grace of the Holy Trinity. The doctrine One God in Trinity is not an abstract philosophical formula. It originates in the personal and corporate experience of the grace of the Triune God which has been and is communicated to us in Jesus Christ. This experience is not to be understood in a merely subjective way. It is rooted in the historic fact of the incarnation and God's revelation of himself in Christ. Doctrine is the attempt to express this revelation in such a way as both to safeguard it from misunderstanding and to enable others to share in it. The formulation of doctrine, which is based on the Scriptures and on a tradition of careful theological reflection, should in no way be seen as an independent intellectual exercise. Ultimately, as St Gregory the Theologian (of Nazianzus) says, 'It is impossible to express God and yet more impossible to conceive him'.[1] Thus doctrinal formulae should in no way detract from the mystery of God which is handed down in the Church from the apostles by the Fathers. It is not the doctrine of the Trinity but the One God in Trinity, the Father, Son and the Holy Spirit, that constitutes the object of Christian worship and faith. Although we may sometimes speak separately of God the Father, sometimes of God the Son and sometimes of God the Holy Spirit, it is always understood that there is no division of one person from another, but all and each reveal in unity the grace and glory of the one Godhead.

37 Christians participate in the grace of the Holy Trinity as members of the Christian community. It is

the Church which is filled by the Holy Spirit and it is precisely for this reason that every human person has the possibility of becoming a partaker of the divine nature (2 Pet. 1.4). The Holy Spirit praying in us heals and renews us at the centre of our being, that is to say in our hearts. The healing character of the grace of the Holy Trinity in the life of the individual believer and of the Church has important implications for the whole life of contemporary society.

Prayer

38   Christian prayer to God is always offered to the Holy Trinity. It is usually addressed to the Father through the Son in the Holy Spirit, although it is also addressed to the Son and sometimes to the Holy Spirit. Although prayer is at one level a human activity, at a deeper level it is the activity in us of God the Holy Spirit, who dwells in our hearts by faith. As St Paul says in Romans 8.26–7: 'Likewise the Spirit helps us in our weakness; for we do not know how to pray as we ought, but the Spirit himself intercedes for us with sighs too deep for words.' So prayer becomes '. . . a possibility by the boundless excellence of the grace of God'.[2]

39   Common to East and West alike is the experience of the Holy Spirit praying in us of which St Paul speaks in Galatians 4.6–7: 'God has sent the Spirit of his Son into our hearts, crying "Abba! Father!"'. So through God you are no longer a slave but a son, and if a son then an heir.' This prayer is described in the Christian tradition in a variety of ways. In Greek patristic writings it is often spoken of as 'prayer of the mind' (νοερὰ προσευχή) where 'mind' is not understood as 'intellect' (in the modern sense) but rather as what St Paul calls 'the heart'. Very similar descriptions of the same experience

of prayer are to be found in early Latin authors like St John Cassian, St Gregory of Tours and St Patrick.[3]

40   In the Eastern Church one of the traditional forms of this prayer is the 'Jesus Prayer'. But prayer of the heart can take other forms, which equally lead to the same experience of the glory of Christ seen and declared by the patriarchs, prophets, apostles, fathers and all the saints.

41   Prayer of the Holy Spirit in the heart of the individual Christian is inseparable from the common liturgical prayer of the Christian community. It is particularly related to the grace given in Baptism, Chrismation (Confirmation) and Eucharist and, generally, to the whole sacramental life of the Church and to common prayer and the reading of Scripture. Both common liturgical prayer and personal prayer are informed and shaped by the Church's faith in God, the Father, the Son and the Holy Spirit.

42   Prayer, both corporate and individual, is an integral part of the life of all Christians. The contemplative and active aspects of Christian life should always be held together, although in the life of each Christian one way or other may predominate at different times, and in the life of some Christians one or the other may predominate throughout their life. For all Christians progress in prayer and obedience involves readiness to take up the cross, and commitment to a disciplined life, whose purpose is their own personal growth in holiness and their more effective witness and service in the Church and in society at large.

Holiness

43   The fruit of the Spirit praying in us is holiness, and

at the heart of holiness is love for God and neighbour. God's love works in us to produce holiness, restoring in us the image of God and making us and all things whole. In this life, Christians experience a tension between the call to holiness and the power of sin, the struggle between 'flesh' and Spirit (Gal. 5.17) which requires continual repentance and the assurance of God's forgiveness. God's call to holiness is also a call to work for justice, so that the Church's prayer for the coming of God's reign on earth as in heaven requires of Christians that they co-operate with God in the world. God's love for the world, embodied in Jesus Christ, works through the Holy Spirit to transfigure all things into the new creation, and we are to make manifest that love in the life of the world.

The *Filioque*

44 Further discussions on the *Filioque* led to the reaffirmation by both Anglicans and Orthodox of the agreement reached in Moscow in 1976 that this phrase should not be included in the Nicene–Constantinopolitan Creed.[4] Certain Anglican Churches have already acted upon this recommendation, whilst others are still considering it.

45 From the theological point of view the Orthodox stated that the doctrine of the *Filioque* is unacceptable, although as expressed by Augustine, it is capable of an Orthodox interpretation. According to the Orthodox understanding the Son cannot be considered a cause or co-cause of the existence of the Holy Spirit. In spite of this we find in certain Fathers, for example St Maximus the Confessor (7th cent.),[5] as explained by Anastasius the Librarian (9th cent.),[6] the opinion that the *Filioque*, as used in early Latin theology, can be understood

in an Orthodox way. According to this interpretation a distinction should be made between two senses of procession, one by which the Father causes the existence of the Spirit (ἐκπόρευσις) and the other by which the Spirit shines forth from the Father *and* the Son (ἔκφανσις). This second sense of procession must be clearly differentiated from the later Western use of the *Filioque* which observed no such distinction but rather confused 'cause of existence' with 'communication of essence' (ἐκπόρευσις) with (ἔκφανσις). Some Orthodox theologians, while affirming that the doctrine of the *Filioque* is unacceptable for the Orthodox Church, at the same time, having in mind the position of Professor Bolotov (1854–1900) and his followers, regard the *Filioque* as a 'theologoumenon' in the West.[7]

46 On the Anglican side it was pointed out that the *Filioque* was not to be regarded as a dogma which would have to be accepted by all Christians. It was emphasized, however, that the following points are important for a correct understanding of its intention:

(*a*) although the Western tradition has spoken from time to time of the Son as a 'cause' (causa) of the Spirit, this language has not met with favour and has fallen into disuse;

(*b*) the Western tradition has continued to maintain that the Father is the sole 'fount of deity' (fons deitatis/πηγὴ Θεότητος) at the same time as it has associated the Son with the Father as the 'principle' (principium) of the Spirit;

(*c*) the Western tradition, in speaking of the Father and the Son as 'one principle', has not meant to imply that the Spirit proceeds from some undifferentiated divine essence (οὐσία), as opposed to the persons (ὑποστάσεις) of the Father and the Son.

The Anglicans on the Commission put on record that

they do not wish to defend the use of the term 'cause' in this context.[8]

NOTES

1   *Theological Orations* II, 4.

2   Origen, *PG* 11, 416A.

3   St John Cassian, *Collations* X, 10.
       St Gregory of Tours, *History of the Franks* V, 10.
       St Patrick, who writes in his *Confession*, chapter 25:

> And another time I saw him praying in me and I was as it were within my body and I heard above me, that is above my inner man, and there he was praying earnestly with groans, and while this was going on I was in amazement and I was wondering and I was considering who it could be who was praying in me but at the end of the prayer he spoke to the effect that it was the Spirit, and at that I woke.

> > Translation in R. P. C. Hanson, *The Life and Writings of The Historical Saint Patrick* (New York 1983), p. 94.

4   Moscow Agreed Statement, Section V 19–21.

5   St Maximus the Confessor, *Letter to Marinos, PG* 91, 133D–136B, *PG* 90, 672 CD.

6   Migne, *PL* 129, 560D–561A.

7   See Archpriest Liveriy Voronov, 'The *Filioque* in the Ecumenical Perspective', in the *Journal of the Moscow Patriarchate* 5 (1982), pp. 66–8; AOJDD.313: L. Voronov, on the Theses of Bolotov; and AOJDD.283: a translation, taken from Professor V.V. Bolotov's book *On the Question of the Filioque* (published in 1914), of his 'Theses on the *Filioque*' together with a passage (pp. 30–6) defining terms, which include Bolotov's own definition of a theologoumenon as follows:

> But I may be asked what I mean by Θεολογούμενον. In essence it is also a theological opinion, but only the opinion of those who for every catholic are more than just theologians: they are the theological opinions of the holy fathers of the one undivided church; they are the opinions of those men, among whom are those who are fittingly called 'ecumenical doctors'. Θεολογούμενα I rate highly, but I do not in any case exaggerate their significance, and I think that I 'quite sharply' distinguish them from dogmas. The content of a dogma is truth: the content of a Θεολογούμενον is only what is probable. The realm of a dogma is necessaria, the realm of a Θεολογούμενον is dubia: In necessariis unitas, in dubiis libertas!

8   For an outline of traditional Anglican views see AOJDD.213, 'The Filioque in Ecumenical Perspective: a preliminary Anglican response', by Professor Eugene Fairweather.

III WORSHIP AND TRADITION

Paradosis – Tradition

47   Looked at from outside, the two Churches appear to be very different in their attitude to tradition, the Anglicans allowing a great variety of attitude and teaching, the Orthodox being strongly attached to the definitions and the structures of the tradition, especially to those established in the Ecumenical Councils and by the Church Fathers.

48   Nevertheless within the freedom existing in the Anglican Communion there is a commitment and responsibility to the tradition, and a conviction that there are elements in the tradition, for instance the historic Creeds and the Chalcedonian definition, of permanent validity. On the Orthodox side, there exists freedom and understanding of tradition as the constant action of the Holy Spirit in the Church, an unceasing presence of the revelation of the Word of God through the Holy Spirit, ever present, here and now. Tradition is always open, ready to embrace the present and accept the future.

49   The Anglicans share this understanding of tradition. Tradition, with Scripture as the normative factor within it (see Moscow Agreed Statement, Section III), is that which maintains our Christian identity, which develops and nurtures our Christian obedience, and makes our Christian witness effective in the power of the Holy Spirit.

50   The tradition of the Church flows from the Father's gift of his Son 'for the life of the world', through the sojourning of the Holy Spirit in the world to be a constant witness to the truth (John 15.26). The Church draws its life and being from this same movement of the

Father's love; that is to say, the Church too lives 'for the life of the world'. Its tradition is the living force and inexhaustible source of its mission to the world.

51   The presence of the Holy Spirit in the Church enables the whole body of the faithful, the *pleroma* of the Church, to be enriched and strengthened in facing the problems of our time, both within the Church and outside it. There is a variety of gifts of the Spirit which work together for the building up of the Christian people for their work of witness and service in the world for the common good. Both Anglicans and Orthodox see in their fidelity to tradition a mutual bond, and a strong incentive to closer co-operation in witness and service to the world.

52   One aspect of the dynamic nature of tradition is to be seen in the way in which the Church assimilates and sanctifies certain elements of the cultures of the various societies in which the Church lives. The Fathers of the Church, under the guidance of the Holy Spirit, exercised a careful discrimination in their use of material from the society around them. The Church at the present time needs to exercise a similar discrimination, remaining true to the mind ($\phi\rho\acute{o}\nu\eta\mu\alpha$) of the Fathers and facing the new questions with which our century confronts us.

Worship and the Maintenance of the Faith

53   Faith and worship are inseparable. Dogmas are not abstract ideas existing in and for themselves, but revealed and saving truths and realities intended to bring mankind into communion with God. Through the liturgical life of the Church creation comes to share in this saving reality. Thus in worship the Church becomes what she really is: body, fellowship, communion in

Christ. She maintains the true faith and is maintained in the truth faith by the action and work of the Holy Spirit.

54 The great affirmations of Christian doctrine have their liturgical formulation and expression; all the saving truths of the faith are doxologically and liturgically appropriated. The Catholic Faith is this, that we worship God, Father, Son and Holy Spirit, Trinity consubstantial and undivided.

55 Liturgy is the action by which the community celebrates the events which created it, sustain it, and give it its future. In both Churches corporate and personal worship are inseparable. It is only as members of the worshipping Church that we can make a true confession of the faith. For example, in the Orthodox Liturgy the Creed is introduced with the words: 'Let us love one another so that with one mind we may confess'. Moreover, because of the nature of man and more especially the incarnation of the Word, the tradition of Christian worship is outward as well as inward, involving bodily gestures and material signs and objects as well as spiritual attitudes.

56 The liturgical life of the Church is the very heart of tradition. The Church in the celebration of its Liturgy recalls the mighty acts of God in the past, experiences them as present and living realities, and anticipates the coming of the Lord in glory. In the presence of the risen Christ we receive the promise of the coming Kingdom. Liturgical time is no cold and lifeless representation of past events, nor simply an historical record. In it Christ himself is living in his Church. Liturgical time is time transfigured through liturgical act, for it is time animated by 'the fervour of faith full of the Holy Spirit' (Liturgy of St John Chrysostom). Thus by

worship we live in the new time of the Kingdom. That implies two things: first, the entrance of the Lord of glory into our history as the Saviour of the world, and second, our entrance into the eternal Kingdom of the Holy Trinity by grace.

57   Liturgy and all Christian worship are rooted in salvation history. Salvation history with all its mighty events in both the Old and New Covenants is confessed, celebrated and appropriated by means of the liturgical year. The centre of that year, as of salvation history itself, is the saving person and work of Jesus Christ present in the power of the Holy Spirit.

58   In the Eucharist we become partakers of the Lord's Supper. The Eucharist is anamnesis and participation in the death and resurrection of Christ, liturgically affirmed and realized in the annual celebration of the Paschal mystery. This is renewed every week in the feast of the Lord's Day and in every celebration of the Holy Eucharist. The fact of the resurrection of Christ is the basis of Christian faith and worship, since as St Paul says: 'If Christ has not been raised . . . your faith is in vain' (1 Cor. 15.14).

59   The significance of the resurrection is liturgically experienced and expressed in the preparatory season of Lent and in the season which follows, from Easter through the Ascension to Pentecost. In the coming of the Paraclete, the whole mystery of Christ is realized: the Holy Spirit takes the things of Christ and shows them to us, making them real in every age; the Paraclete is thus the constant source of life in the tradition of the Church.

60   The Church baptizes her members into the death and resurrection of her Lord, bringing them from the state of sin and death into membership of his body and

participation in his eternal life. The centrality of the Easter solemnity has made Easter the supreme occasion for the administration of the rites of Christian initiation.

61   As in the divine economy of salvation, the atonement achieved by the death and resurrection of Christ presupposes the incarnation and the incarnate life of Christ, so in the Christian year, the feast of Easter presupposes the feasts of the Nativity and the Epiphany and the other feasts related to the life of our Saviour. Thus we have the yearly cycle of the feasts of our Lord. In the West the season of Advent prepares Christians to celebrate Christ's coming as Saviour, and reminds them of his future coming in judgement and glory.

62   Finally the liturgical year includes the feasts of the Blessed Virgin Mary, Mother of God, and of the Saints, witnessing thus to the dogmatic truth that Christ the head of the Church remains always united with the members of his body and that there is no separation between the militant and triumphant Church. 'The Lord is wonderful in his Saints', and in the communion of the saints we see again the power of the resurrection in the life and tradition of the Church destroying death and transfiguring time.

63   Anglicans and Orthodox hold that the liturgy and all worship are essentially for the expression, maintenance and communication of the true faith. Liturgical texts are thus fundamental doctrinal standards for both. Both recognize the possibility of the Church making liturgical revisions according to the necessity of the times, and with a view to the salvation of the people of God. They differ only in their estimation of the need for such revisions in the present situation, this difference reflecting their diverse historical experiences and situations.

64   In both Anglican and Orthodox traditions, prayers and devotions in the family are understood as an extension of the corporate worship of the Church. From New Testament times onwards the Christian family has been considered to be a household church. The rite of marriage, a sign or image of the spiritual union between Christ and his Church, initiates a relationship within which children may be nurtured and where the faith is taught, lived, and communicated to others.

65   The traditions of both Churches are rich in a variety of family devotions and customs which include the use of parts of the Divine Office, reverence of icons, use of crosses and pictures, grace at meals, Bible reading, as well as blessings of events and turning points of family life. Both Anglican and Orthodox members are convinced of the importance of the family and the household church as a vehicle of the tradition of the Church and wish to explore this further.

The Communion of Saints and the Departed

66   All prayer is ultimately addressed to the Triune God. We pray to God the Father through our Lord Jesus Christ in the Holy Spirit. The Church is united in a single movement of worship with the Church in heaven, with the Blessed Virgin Mary, 'with angels and archangels, and all the company of heaven'. The Orthodox also pray to the Blessed Virgin Mary and Theotokos and the saints as friends and living images of Christ.

67   Those who believe and are baptized form one body in Christ, and are members one of another, united by the Holy Spirit. Within the Body each member suffers and rejoices with the others, and in each member the Holy Spirit intercedes for the whole. These relationships are changed but not broken by death. 'He is not God of

the dead, but of the living' (Matt. 22.32), for all live in and to him. This is the meaning of the communion of saints.

68   God is 'the God of Abraham, the God of Isaac, and the God of Jacob' (Exod. 3.6), 'the Lord of hosts' (Isa. 6.3), 'the God and Father of our Lord Jesus Christ' (Rom. 15.6). Our God is not an abstract idea, but the God of persons, revealing himself in and to particular men and women. Union with God therefore involves us in a personal relationship with all who belong to him through the grace of the Holy Spirit who both unites and diversifies: and this personal relationship, which is not broken by death, is precisely the communion of saints.

69   Our experience of the communion of saints finds its fullest expression in the Eucharist, in which the whole Body of Christ realizes its unity in the Holy Spirit. We see this in ancient eucharistic prayers of East and West, which commemorate the saints and intercede for the departed as well as for the living.

70   'Christ is risen from the dead trampling down death by death. . . ' By virtue of Christ's cross and resurrection, death is no longer an impassable barrier. It is this sense of our continuing union in the risen Christ that forms for all Orthodox the basis of prayer for the dead and the invocation of the saints. Mainly as a result of the abuses of the medieval West, and the consequent Reformation in the sixteenth century, Anglicans rejected much of the practice and teaching of the Church of that time. The cult of the saints and prayer for the departed were criticized on the grounds of the all-sufficiency of Christ's redeeming work. Today there is a variety of practice among Anglicans on these matters. All remain careful in the language which they use in prayer for the

departed, being anxious not to return to the errors of the Western Middle Ages. But all affirm our union with the departed in the risen Christ.

71   God's love is present everywhere and is offered to everybody, but not everyone accepts it. According to some Fathers, even those in hell are not deprived of the love of God but by their own free choice they experience as torment what the saints experience as joy. The light of God's glory is also the fire of judgement. God's wrath is no other than his love; how we experience that love, in this life and after death, depends on our attitude. The Orthodox Church in the prayers of Pentecost, believing that Christ has the keys of death and hell (Rev. 1.18), and hoping that the love of God will find a response in the souls even of some who are in hell, prays for their salvation, although their ultimate destiny remains a mystery (Matt. 25.31–46 as understood by the Fathers).[1]

72   ' . . . from one degree of glory to another' (2 Cor. 3.18): for the righteous, in the view of the Orthodox and also of many Anglicans, further progress and growth in the love of God will continue for ever. After death, this progress is to be thought of in terms of healing rather than satisfaction or retribution. Other Anglicans think of perfection in Christ as an immediate gift in the life to come. As Anglicans and Orthodox we are agreed in rejecting any doctrine of purgatory which suggests that the departed through their sufferings are making 'satisfaction' or 'expiation' for their sins. The traditional practice of the Church in praying for the faithful departed is to be understood as an expression of the unity between the Church militant and the Church triumphant, and of the love which one bears to the other.

73   Prayers for the departed are therefore to be seen,

not in juridical terms, but as an expression of mutual love and solidarity in Christ: 'we pray for them because we still hold them in our love' (Catechism of the Episcopal Church, USA).

74   The prayers of the saints on our behalf are likewise to be understood as an expression of mutual love and shared life in the Holy Spirit. Such a term as 'treasury of merits' is foreign to both our traditions. 'There is one God, and there is one mediator between God and men, the man Christ Jesus' (1 Tim. 2.5): the intercession of the saints for us is always in and through this unique mediation of Christ. The saints reign with Christ (cf. Luke 22.29–30): Christ is the King, and the saints share in his kingly rule.

75   The Blessed Virgin Mary played a unique role in the economy of salvation by virtue of the fact that she was chosen to be Mother of Christ our God. Her intercession is not autonomous, but presupposes Christ's intercession and is based upon the saving work of the incarnate Word.

76   The Orthodox practice of commemorating the saints of the Old Testament powerfully affirms the way in which the whole history of salvation is made present in the liturgy of the Church.

77   All Anglican liturgies refer to the communion of saints by thanking God for that communion and for the lives and examples of particular saints, and some refer to the saints' prayers for us, but very few contain invocations addressed directly to saints.

78   Much of the language in which we speak of the saints and the departed is derived from the life of prayer and piety. Many of the Church's affirmations concerning the communion of saints are in hymnography and

iconography. At the same time there is an appropriate doctrinal reserve which reflects the mystery of our relationship with the departed. It is in God alone that we have communion with them.

Icons

79   In the incarnation human nature, body as well as soul, was assumed into the life of the Word of God; and in the renewed creation, which this incarnation has effected, the whole material world is sanctified, and the destructive opposition of matter and spirit overcome.

80   In the Orthodox tradition the depiction and use of icons has a christological foundation. The icon is understood as an important means whereby we confess and appropriate the mystery of the incarnation.

81   Anglicans have in the past felt serious difficulties about this question. For example a committee of the Lambeth Conference in 1888 said: 'It would be difficult for us to enter more intimate relations with that (sc. Orthodox) Church as long as it retains the use of icons.' These difficulties are part of a larger history of the West. The decrees of the Seventh Ecumenical Council were not properly understood in the West owing to the unfortunate translation of the Greek word προσκύνησις (veneration) by the Latin word *adoratio* (worship). The subsequent uncontrolled development of visual imagery later in the Middle Ages in the West led to strong reactions, above all at the time of the Reformation. The Reformers understood the prohibition of idolatry in the Ten Commandments as applying to the practices of their own day. They sought to purify and simplify the worship of the Church, in order that glory might be given to God alone. In particular they rejected the worship of images.

82   Anglicans however did not reject all use of bodily gestures and images in the worship of the Church. The Book of Common Prayer retains, for example, the use of the sign of the cross in Baptism, and the giving of a ring in marriage. In the controversies in the century following the Reformation, Anglicans constantly appealed to the words of St Paul, 'All things should be done decently and in order' (1 Cor. 14.40). In his exposition of the Church Catechism, *The Practice of Divine Love*, Bishop Thomas Ken (1637–1711) prays, 'give me grace to pay a religious, suitable veneration to all sacred persons or places or things which are thine by solemn dedication and separated for the uses of divine love, and the communications of thy grace, or which may promote the decency and order of the worship, or the edification of faithful people'. In fact a distinctive Anglican tradition of religious art developed. During the last hundred years increasing contact with the Orthodox Churches and a fuller knowledge of their tradition have brought new light to this question.

83   In the light of the present discussion the Anglicans do not find any cause for disagreement in the doctrine as stated by St John of Damascus: 'In times past, God, without body and form could in no way be represented. But now since God has appeared in flesh and lived among men, I can depict that which is visible of God. I do not venerate matter, but I venerate the creator of matter, who became matter for me, who condescended to live in matter, and who through matter accomplished my salvation; and I do not cease to respect the matter through which my salvation is accomplished.'[2]

84   By the incarnation of the Word who is the image of the Father (2 Cor. 4.4; Col. 1.15; Heb. 1.3) the image of God in every man is restored and the material world itself sanctified and again made capable of mediating

the divine beauty. Icons are used as a means of expressing, as far as it can be expressed, the glory of God seen
in the face of Jesus Chirst (2 Cor. 4.6), and in the faces
of his friends. Icons are words in painting, referring to
the history of salvation and its manifestation in specific
persons. Icons have always been understood as a visible
gospel, as a testimony to the great things given to us
by God the Word incarnate. In the Council of 860 it was
stated that 'all that is uttered in words written in syl-
lables is also proclaimed in the language of colours'.
From this perspective icons and Scripture are linked
through an inner relationship; both coexist in the
Church and proclaim the same truths. 'Just as in the
Bible we listen to the word of Christ and are sanctified
. . . in the same way through the painted icons we
behold the representation of his human form . . . and
are likewise sanctified' (St John of Damascus).[3]

85 An icon is a means of entering into contact with
the person or event it represents. It is not an end in
itself. In the words of St Basil: 'The honour shown to
the icon passes to the prototype'.[4] It guides us to a
vision of the divine Kingdom where past, present and
future are one. It makes vivid our faith in the communion of the saints. In the definition of the Seventh Ecumenical Council we read: 'The more frequently they
(sc. icons) are seen, the more those who behold them
are aroused to remember and desire the prototypes and
to give them greeting and the veneration of honour; not
indeed true worship which, according to our faith, is
due to God alone.'[5]

86 Just as Scripture is understood within the community of faith, so too the icon is understood within
the same community of faith and worship. It is an essentially liturgical form of art. In response to the faith and
prayer of the believers, God, through the icon, bestows

his sanctifying and healing grace. Thus the icon serves to promote the communication of the gospel and hence its making and use must always be controlled by theological criteria. It is not a random decoration, but an integral part of the Church's life and worship. In this respect its place in the Church's worship can be compared with the place of music and chant and with the faithful preaching of the word of God.

87   In our time, when visual imagery plays a more and more important part in people's lives, the tradition of icons has acquired a startling relevance. It presents the Church with a new possibility of proclaiming the gospel in a society in which language is often devalued.

NOTES

1   Eg. *PG* 57–8, 717ff.
2   On Holy Icons I, *PG* 94, 1245B.
3   On Holy Icons III, *PG* 94, 1333D.
4   On Holy Spirit 18, *PG* 32, 149 C8f.
5   Mansi, *Concilia* XIII, 482.

EPILOGUE

88   At this point in our work, after twelve years of discussion, we feel it right to attempt a summary of the progress that, as Anglicans and Orthodox, we have been able to achieve with God's help. We note in particular the following points over which we agree or disagree, or which we see as requiring further exploration:

I The Knowledge of God

89   Here we have discovered a difference in terminology, but no difference in fundamental belief. The normal Orthodox ways of speaking about the essence and energies of God, and about 'divinization' ($\Theta\acute{\epsilon}\omega\sigma\iota\varsigma$), are not employed by most Anglicans, but Anglicans do not reject the underlying doctrine which this language expresses.[1]

II Scripture and Tradition

90   (a) We agree in our basic understanding of the inspiration and authority of Scripture, and we agree more particularly that the Church gives attention to the results of scholarly research concerning the Bible. But we have not attempted to state in detail how critical methods of historical research are to be applied to the Bible, for we see this as a task outside the scope of a commission such as our own. We have noted a minor difference over the distinction which both Churches make between the canonical books of the Old Testament and the deutero-canonical books: the Orthodox Church has not pronounced officially on the nature of the distinction, as is done in the Articles of the Church of England.[2]

91 (*b*) We agree likewise in our view of the fundamental relationship between Scripture and tradition: they are not two sources, but correlative. We agree that the Church cannot define dogmas which are not grounded both in Scripture and in tradition. We agree that the 'mind' (φρόνημα) of the Fathers is of lasting importance for our understanding of the Christian faith.

92 We agree that tradition is to be seen in dynamic terms, as the constant action of the Holy Spirit in the Church; and therefore both our delegations accept that there exist freedom and variety within the one tradition of the Church. But we have not yet attempted to state in detail what are the limits of that freedom and variety in regard to every specific point of doctrine.[3]

III The Holy Trinity

93 (*a*) We agree in affirming that prayer and sanctification are founded upon the grace of the Holy Trinity.[4]

94 (*b*) We agree that the original form of the Nicene–Constantinopolitan Creed referred to the origin of the Holy Spirit from the Father. For this reason, and because the *Filioque* was introduced into the Creed without the authority of an Ecumenical Council and without due regard to catholic consent, the Anglicans agree with the Orthodox that the *Filioque* should not be included in the Creed.[5]

95 (*c*) We have discussed how far the doctrine implied by the *Filioque* (as distinguished from the inclusion of the *Filioque* in the Creed) is acceptable to our two churches. Here we have failed to reach full agreement. The Anglican delegates regard the *Filioque* as a valid theological statement, though not as a dogma. The Orthodox delegates regard the doctrine of the *Filioque*

as unacceptable, but they note that according to some Eastern Fathers, the use of the *Filioque* in early Latin theology can be understood in an Orthodox way.[6]

IV The Church

96 (*a*) We agree in our fundamental understanding of the Church as one, holy, catholic and apostolic.[7]

97 (*b*) Despite differences in the outward forms of wider leadership within our two Communions, there is fundamental agreement between the way in which Anglicans understand 'primacy' and the way in which Orthodox understand 'seniority'. We agree more particularly that all levels of wider leadership within the Church are to be envisaged in terms not of coercion but of pastoral service.[8]

98 (*c*) We agree in our basic understanding of witness, evangelism and service within the Church. More especially we affirm that missionary witness to unbelievers, and sacrificial service to those in need, are the shared responsibility of all church members, clergy and lay people alike.[9]

99 (*d*) But while we agree that the Church is one, holy, catholic and apostolic, we are not agreed on the account to be given of the sinfulness and division which is to be observed in the life of Christian communities. For Anglicans, because the Church under Christ is the community where God's grace is at work, healing and transforming sinful men and women; and because grace in the Church is mediated through those who are themselves undergoing such transformation, the struggle between grace and sin is to be seen as characteristic of, rather than accidental to, the Church on earth. Orthodox, while agreeing that the human members of the Church on earth are sinful, do not believe that sinfulness

should be ascribed to the Church as the body of Christ indwelt by the Holy Spirit.

100   (*e*) As regards the first of the four marks of the Church, its oneness, we disagree in our view of the relationship between the Church's basic unity and the present state of division between Christians. The Anglican members see our divisions as existing within the Church while the Orthodox members believe that the Orthodox Church is the one true Church of Christ, which as his Body is not and cannot be divided.[10]

101   (*f*) With this is linked a further disagreement, concerning communion and intercommunion. The Anglican tradition accepts as legitimate, in certain situations, the use of intercommunion as a means towards the attainment of full organic unity. The Orthodox reject the notion of intercommunion, and believe that there can be communion only between local churches that have a unity of faith, ministry and sacraments.[11]

102   (*g*) As regards the fourth of the four marks of the Church, its apostolicity, we agree that this is manifested in a particular way through the succession of bishops and that this succession is a sign of the unbroken continuity of apostolic tradition and life.[12] But we have not so far discussed what is the attitude of our two Churches towards such communities as have not preserved the succession of bishops in an outward and visible form. Nor have we discussed the Orthodox view of the validity of Anglican ordinations.

103   (*h*) We have failed to reach agreement concerning the possibility, or otherwise, of the ordination of women to the priesthood. The Orthodox affirm that such ordination is impossible, since it is contrary to Scripture and tradition. With this some Anglicans agree, while

others believe that it is possible, and even desirable at the present moment, to ordain women as priests.[13] There are, however, many related issues that we have not so far examined in any detail, particularly the following: how we are to understand the distinction within humanity between man and woman; what is meant by sacramental priesthood, and how this is related to the unique high priesthood of Christ and to the royal priesthood of all the baptized; what, apart from the sacramental priesthood, are the other forms of ministry within the Church.

V Councils

104 (a) We agree that the Ecumenical Councils provide an authoritative interpretation of Scripture in order to safeguard the salvation of the People of God.

105 (b) We differ, however, in our understanding of the relative importance of the Councils. While the Anglican members lay greater emphasis upon the first four Councils, and less upon the fifth, sixth and seventh, applying to conciliar decisions the concept of an 'order' or 'hierarchy of truths', the Orthodox members find this concept to be in conflict with the unity of the faith as a whole.

106 (c) We are agreed in considering that infallibility is not the property of any particular person in the Church. But we consider that the implications of the terms 'infallible' and 'indefectible' need to be further explored.

107 (d) We are agreed that the ecumenicity of Councils is manifested through their acceptance by the Church. But we feel that further discussion is needed of the processes whereby the teaching of Councils is recognized and accepted.[14]

VI Faith and Worship, Church and Eucharist

108 (*a*) We are agreed about the integral link between faith and worship, between the tradition of the Church and its liturgical life. We are agreed in our general understanding of baptism, although we have not discussed this in detail. We are agreed in describing the Eucharist as an *anamnesis* and participation in the death and resurrection of Christ.[15]

109 (*b*) We are agreed in regarding the Church as a eucharistic community: the Eucharist actualizes the Church. In each local eucharistic celebration the visible unity and catholicity of the Church is fully manifested. The question of the relationship between the celebrant and his bishop and that among bishops themselves requires further study.[16]

110 (*c*) We are agreed in attaching cardinal importance to the action of the Holy Spirit in the Eucharist, as also throughout the entire life of the Church. In the Orthodox eucharistic liturgy this is an invocation (ἐπίκλησις) of the Holy Spirit; in some Anglican liturgies there is no such explicit *epiclesis*, but all Anglicans are agreed that the operation of the Holy Spirit is essential to the Eucharist.[17]

111 (*d*) We are agreed that through the consecratory prayer, addressed to the Father, the bread and wine become the Body and Blood of the glorified Christ by the action of the Holy Spirit in such a way that the faithful people of God receiving Christ may feed upon him in the sacrament.[18] But we have not yet discussed in detail what is the nature of the ineffable change effected through the consecratory prayer, nor have we considered how far the Eucharist may be regarded as a sacrifice.[19]

112   (*e*) We have reached basic agreement on the communion of saints and the departed. All of us believe that the communion of the Holy Spirit joins in unity the members of the Body, whether living or departed, and this unity is expressed in prayer and thanksgiving. There remains, however, a certain difference here between Orthodoxy and Anglicanism, since in most Anglican Churches, requests to the saints to pray for us are not made, and also prayers for the faithful departed, though common, are by no means universal; and some Anglicans believe that only thanksgiving for the departed is appropriate. Moreover, not all Anglicans agree with the Orthodox Patristic understanding of endless progress after death.[20]

113   (*f*) In regard to icons we have found that notwithstanding past Anglican objections and despite differences in liturgical practice, there is no serious disagreement here between Anglicanism and Orthodoxy. It is true that Anglicans do not believe that the veneration of icons, as practised in the East, can be required of all Christians. But Anglicans agree that the theology of the icon is founded upon, and intended to safeguard, the doctrine of the incarnation. They also accept that it is legitimate to regard the icon, not merely as a decoration, but as a means of entering into relationship with the person or event it represents; and to hold that in response to the faith and prayer of the believers, God through the icon, bestows his sanctifying grace. We have not yet adequately discussed the difference between two- and three-dimensional images.[21]

114   None of the points of disagreement mentioned above is to be regarded as insoluble, but each is to be regarded as a challenge to this Commission, or to some similar body to be appointed in the future by our two Churches, to advance more deeply in its understanding

of the truth. Anglicans and Orthodox alike, we are called to 'reach out towards that which lies ahead, pressing forward to win the prize which is God's call to the life above, in Christ Jesus' (Phil. 3.13–14).

NOTES

1   Moscow Agreed Statement para. 1–3.
2   MAS para. 4–8.
3   MAS para. 9–12; Dublin Agreed Statement para. 47–52.
4   DAS para. 36–43.
5   MAS para. 19–21.
6   DAS para. 44–6.
7   DAS para. 2–17.
8   DAS para. 21–30.
9   DAS para. 31–5.
10   DAS para. 8–9.
11   DAS para. 18–20.
12   DAS para. 14–17.
13   DAS Appendix 2.
14   MAS para. 13–18; DAS para. 29–30.
15   DAS para. 53–65.
16   MAS para. 22–7.
17   MAS para. 29–32.
18   MAS para. 25–6.
19   MAS para. 22 refers to the Bucharest Statement of 1935 on the Eucharist, which is printed with an introduction on pp. 92–3 of *Anglican–Orthodox Dialogue: Moscow Agreed Statement* (SPCK 1977). However we have not discussed it in detail, nor, acting as a Joint Commission, have we as yet expressed our agreement or otherwise with the six points that it contains.
20   DAS para. 66–78.
21   DAS para. 79–87; MAS para. 15.

APPENDIX 1
THE MOSCOW AGREED STATEMENT 1976

I The Knowledge of God

1   God is both immanent and transcendent. By virtue of the divine self-revelation, man experiences personal communion with God. By faith and through obedience he shares truly in the divine life and is united with God the Holy Trinity. By grace he enjoys the pledge and first-fruits of eternal glory. But, however close this union may be, there remains always an all-important distinction between God and man, Creator and creature, infinite and finite.

2   To safeguard both the transcendence of God and the possibility of man's true union with him the Orthodox Church draws a distinction between the divine essence, which remains for ever beyond man's comprehension and knowledge, and the divine energies, by participation in which man participates in God. The divine energies are God himself in his self-manifestation. This distinction is not normally used by Anglicans, but in various ways they also seek to express the belief that God is at once incomprehensible, yet truly knowable by man.

3   To describe the fullness of man's sanctification and the way in which he shares in the life of God, the Orthodox Church uses the Patristic term *theosis kata charin* (divinization by grace). Once again such language is not normally used by Anglicans, some of whom regard it as misleading and dangerous. At the same time Anglicans recognize that, when Orthodox speak in this manner, they do so only with the most careful safeguards. Anglicans do not reject the underlying doctrine which this language seeks to express; indeed, such teaching is to be found in their own liturgies and hymnody.

II The Inspiration and Authority of Holy Scripture

4   The Scriptures constitute a coherent whole. They are at once divinely inspired and humanly expressed. They bear authoritative witness to God's revelation of himself in creation, in the Incarnation of the Word and in the whole history of salvation, and as such express the Word of God in human language

5 We know, receive, and interpret Scripture through the Church and in the Church. Our approach to the Bible is one of obedience so that we may hear the revelation of himself that God gives through it.

6 The books of Scripture contained in the Canon are authoritative because they truly convey the authentic revelation of God, which the Church recognizes in them. Their authority is not determined by any particular theories concerning the authorship of these books or the historical circumstances in which they were written. The Church gives attention to the results of scholarly research concerning the Bible from whatever quarter they come, but it tests them in the light of its experience and understanding of the faith as a whole.

7 The Church believes in the apostolic origin of the New Testament, as containing the witness of those who had seen the Lord.

8 Both the Orthodox and the Anglican Churches make a distinction between the canonical books of the Old Testament and the deutero-canonical books (otherwise called the *Anaginoskomena*) although the Orthodox Churches have not pronounced officially on the nature of the distinction, as is done in the Anglican Articles. Both Communions are agreed in regarding the deutero-canonical books as edifying and both, and in particular the Orthodox Church, make liturgical use of them.

III Scripture and Tradition

9 Any disjunction between Scripture and Tradition such as would treat them as two separate 'sources of revelation' must be rejected. The two are correlative. We affirm (i) that Scripture is the main criterion whereby the Church tests traditions to determine whether they are truly part of Holy Tradition or not; (ii) that Holy Tradition completes Holy Scripture in the sense that it safeguards the integrity of the biblical message.

10 (i) By the term Holy Tradition we understand the entire life of the Church in the Holy Spirit. This tradition expresses itself in dogmatic teaching, in liturgical worship, in canonical discipline, and in spiritual life. These elements together manifest the single and indivisible life of the Church.

(ii) Of supreme importance is the dogmatic tradition, which in substance is unchangeable. In seeking to communicate the saving truth to mankind, the Church in every generation makes use of contemporary language and therefore of contemporary modes of thought; but this usage must always be tested by the standard of Scripture and of the dogmatic definitions of the Ecumenical Councils. The mind (*phronema*) of the Fathers, their theological method, their terminology and modes of expression have a lasting importance in both the Orthodox and the Anglican Churches.

(iii) The liturgical and canonical expressions of Tradition can differ, in that they are concerned with varying situations of the people of God in different historical periods and in different places. The liturgical and canonical traditions remain unchangeable to the extent that they embody the unchangeable truth of divine revelation and respond to the unchanging needs of mankind.

11   The Church cannot define dogmas which are not grounded both in Holy Scripture and in Holy Tradition, but has the power, particularly in Ecumenical Councils, to formulate the truths of the faith more exactly and precisely when the needs of the Church require it.

12   The understanding of Scripture and Tradition embodied in paragraphs 4 to 11 offers to our Churches a solid basis for closer rapprochement.

IV The Authority of the Council

13   We are agreed that the notions of Church and Scripture are inseparable. The Scriptures contain the witness of the prophets and apostles to the revelation of himself which God the Father made to man through his Son in his Holy Spirit. The Councils maintain this witness and provide an authoritative interpretation of it. We recognize the work of the Holy Spirit in the Church not only in the Scriptures, but also in the Councils, and in the whole process whereby Scriptures and Councils have been received as authoritative. At the same time we confess that the tradition of the Church is a living one in which the Spirit continues his work of maintaining the true witness to the Revelation of God, the faith once delivered to the saints.

14   We note that Anglican members, while accepting the dog-

matic degrees of the fifth, sixth, and seventh Councils, have long been accustomed to lay more emphasis on the first four, and believe that the concept of 'an order or "hierarchy" of truths' can usefully be applied to the decisions of the Councils. The Orthodox members find this concept to be in conflict with the unity of the faith as a whole, though they recognize gradations of importance in matters of practice.

15   The Orthodox regard the Seventh Council as of equal importance with the other Ecumenical Councils. They understand its positive injunctions about the veneration of icons as an expression of faith in the Incarnation.

The Anglican tradition places a similarly positive value on the created order, and on the place of the body and material things in worship. Like the Orthodox, Anglicans see this as a necessary corollary of the doctrine of the Incarnation. They welcome the decisions of the Seventh Council in so far as they constitute a defence of the doctrine of the Incarnation. They agree that the veneration of icons as practised in the East is not to be rejected, but do not believe that it can be required of all Christians.

It is quite clear that further discussion of the Seventh Council and of icons is necessary in the dialogue between Orthodox and Anglicans, as also of Western three-dimensional images and religious paintings which we have not adequately discussed.

16   We are agreed that according to the Scriptures and the Fathers the fullness of saving truth has been given to the Church. She is the Temple of God, in which God's Spirit dwells, the Pillar and the Ground of truth. Christ has promised that he will be with her until the End of the Age and the Holy Spirit will guide her into all truth (1 Cor. 3.16; 1 Tim. 3.15; Matt. 28.20; John 16.13).

17   Both Anglican and Orthodox agree that infallibility is not the property of any particular institution or person in the Church, but that the promises of Christ are made to the whole Church. The ecumenicity of Councils is manifested through their acceptance by the Church. For the Orthodox, the Ecumenical Council is not an institution but a charismatic event in the life of the Church and is the highest expression of the Church's inerrancy.

18   It is clear that further exploration and discussion of this and

kindred questions will be needed. Among the points to be taken into account are:

(a) The use of the words 'infallible' and 'indefectible' in discussion of ecclesiology is of medieval and modern Western origin.

(b) For Anglicans, the concept of infallibility has acquired unfortunate associations by reason of the definition of the First Vatican Council, and of the manner in which papal authority has been exercised. For the Orthodox, the concept of indefectibility has ambiguous associations on account of the way in which it has been used in modern theology.

(c) A theological evaluation is required of processes whereby the teaching of Councils has been recognized and received.

V The *Filioque* Clause

19   The question of the *Filioque* is in the first instance a question of the content of the Creed, i.e. the summary of the articles of faith which are to be confessed by all. In the Nicaeno-Constantinopolitan Creed (commonly called the Nicene Creed) of 381 the words 'proceeding from the Father' are an assertion of the divine origin and nature of the Holy Spirit, parallel to the assertion of the divine origin and nature of the Son contained in the words 'begotten not made, consubstantial with the Father'. The word *ekporeuomenon* (proceeding), as used in the Creed, denotes the incomprehensible mode of the Spirit's origin from the Father, employing the language of Scripture (John 15.26). It asserts that the Spirit comes from the Father in a manner which is not that of generation.

20   The question of the origin of the Holy Spirit is to be distinguished from that of his mission to the world. It is with reference to the mission of the Spirit that we are to understand the biblical texts which speak both of the Father (John 14.26) and of the Son (John 15.26) as sending (*pempein*) the Holy Spirit.

21   The Anglican members therefore agree that:

(a) because the original form of the Creed referred to the origin of the Holy Spirit from the Father,

(b) because the *Filioque* clause was introduced into this Creed without the authority of an Ecumenical Council and without due regard for Catholic consent, and

(c) because this Creed constitutes the public confession of faith by the People of God in the Eucharist,

the *Filioque* clause should not be included in this Creed.

VI The Church as the Eucharistic Community

22   The eucharistic teaching and practice of the Churches, mutually confessed, constitutes an essential factor for the understanding which can lead to reunion between the Orthodox and Anglican Churches. This understanding commits both our Churches to a close relationship which can provide the basis for further steps on the way to reconciliation and union. Already in the past there has been considerable agreement between representatives of our two Churches regarding the doctrine of the Eucharist. We note particularly the six points of the Bucharest Conference of 1935. We now report the following points of agreement:

23   The eucharistic understanding of the Church affirms the presence of Jesus Christ in the Church, which is his Body, and in the Eucharist. Through the action of the Holy Spirit, all faithful communicants share in the one Body of Christ, and become one body in him.

24   The Eucharist actualizes the Church. The Christian community has a basic sacramental character. The Church can be described as a *synaxis* or an *ecclesia*, which is, in its essence, a worshipping and eucharistic assembly. The Church is not only built up by the Eucharist, but is also a condition for it. Therefore one must be a believing member of the Church in order to receive the Holy Communion.

The Church celebrating the Eucharist becomes fully itself; that is *koinonia*, fellowship – communion. The Church celebrates the Eucharist as the central act of its existence, in which the ecclesial community, as a living reality confessing its faith, receives its realization.

25   Through the consecratory prayer, addressed to the Father, the bread and wine become the Body and Blood of the glorified Christ by the action of the Holy Spirit in such a way that the faithful people of God receiving Christ may feed upon him in the sacrament (1 Cor. 10.16). Thus the Church depends upon the action of the Holy Spirit and is the visible community in which

the Spirit is known.

26   The eucharistic action of the Church is the Passover from the old to the new. It anticipates and really shares in the eternal Rule and Glory of God. Following the Apostolic and Patristic teaching, we affirm that the eucharistic elements become, by the grace of the Holy Spirit, the Body and Blood of Christ, the bread of immortality, to give to us the forgiveness of sins, the new creation, and eternal life. The celebration of the Church in liturgy carries with it the sense of the eternal reality which precedes it, abides in it, and is still to come.

27   In the Eucharist the eternal priesthood of Christ is constantly manifested in time. The celebrant, in his liturgical action, has a twofold ministry: as an icon of Christ, acting in the name of Christ, towards the community and also as a representative of the community expressing the priesthood of the faithful. In each local eucharistic celebration the visible unity and catholicity of the Church is manifested fully. The question of the relationship between the celebrant and his bishop and that among bishops themselves requires further study.

28   The Eucharist impels the believers to specific action in mission and service to the world. In the eucharistic celebration the Church is a confessing community which witnesses to the cosmic transfiguration. Thus God enters into a personal historic situation as the Lord of creation and of history. In the Eucharist the End breaks into our midst, bringing the judgement and hope of the New Age. The final dismissal or benediction in the liturgy is not an end to worship but a call to prayer and witness so that in the power of the Holy Spirit the believers may announce and convey to the world that which they have seen and received in the Eucharist.

VII The Invocation of the Holy Spirit in the Eucharist

29   The Eucharist is the action of the Holy Trinity. The Father gives the Body and the Blood of Christ by the descent of the Holy Spirit to the Church in response to the Church's prayer. The Liturgy is this prayer for the eucharistic gifts to be given. It is in this context that the invocation of the Holy Spirit should be understood. The operation of the Holy Spirit is essential to the

Eucharist whether it is explicitly expressed or not. When it is articulated, the 'Epiclesis' voices the work of the Spirit with the Father in the consecration of the elements as the Body and Blood of Christ.

30   The consecration of the bread and the wine results from the whole sacramental liturgy. The act of consecration includes certain proper and appropriate moments – thanksgiving, anamnesis, *Epiclesis*. The deepest understanding of the hallowing of the elements rejects any theory of consecration by formula – whether by Words of Institution or *Epiclesis*.[1] For the Orthodox the culminating and decisive moment in the consecration is the *Epiclesis*.

31   The unity of the members of the Church is renewed by the Spirit in the eucharistic act. The Spirit comes not only upon the elements, but upon the community. The *Epiclesis* is a double invocation: by the invocation of the Spirit, the members of Christ are fed by his Body and Blood so that they may grow in holiness and may be strong to manifest Christ to the world and to do his work in the power of the Spirit. 'We hold this treasure in earthen vessels.' The reception of the Holy Gifts calls for repentance and obedience. Christ judges the sinful members of the Church. The time is always at hand when judgement must begin at the household of God (2 Cor. 4.7; 1 Pet. 4.17).

32   Although *Epiclesis* has a special meaning in the Eucharist, we must not restrict the concept to the Eucharist alone. In every sacrament, prayer and blessing the Church invokes the Holy Spirit and in all these various ways calls upon him to sanctify the whole creation. The Church is that Community which lives by continually invoking the Holy Spirit.

NOTE

1   At their meeting in Thessaloniki in April 1977 the Orthodox members asked that it should be pointed out that, in regard to the words in paragraph 30 of the Moscow Agreed Statement it is inexact to call the *Epiclesis* a 'formula' since the Orthodox Church does not regard it as such.

APPENDIX 2
THE ATHENS REPORT 1978

The Report of the special meeting of the Anglican–Orthodox Joint Doctrinal Commission held in Athens in July 1978 included the following sections:

III The Orthodox position on the ordination of women to the Priesthood

The Orthodox members of the Commission unanimously affirm the following:

(1) God created mankind in his image as male and female, establishing a diversity of functions and gifts. These functions are complementary but, as St Paul insists (1 Cor. 12), not all are interchangeable. In the life of the Church, as in that of the family, God has assigned certain tasks and forms of ministry specifically to the man, and others – different, yet no less important – to the woman. There is every reason for Christians to oppose current trends which make men and women interchangeable in their functions and roles, and thus lead to the dehumanization of life.

(2) The Orthodox Church honours a woman, the Holy Virgin Mary, the Theotokos, as the human person closest to God. In the Orthodox tradition women saints are given such titles as *megalomartys* (great martyr) and *isapostolos* (equal to the apostles). Thus it is clear that in no sense does the Orthodox Church consider women to be intrinsically inferior in God's eyes. Men and women are equal but different, and we need to recognize this diversity of gifts. Both in discussion among themselves and in dialogue with other Christians, the Orthodox recognize the duty of the Church to give women more opportunities to use their specific *charismata* (gifts) for the benefit of the whole people of God. Among the ministries (*diakoniai*) exercised by women in the Church we note the following;

39   (i) ministries of a diaconal and philanthropic kind, involving the pastoral care of the sick and needy, of refugees and many others, and issuing in various forms of social responsibility.

(ii) ministries of prayer and intercession, of spiritual help and guidance, particularly but not exclusively in connection with the monastic communities,

(iii) ministries connected with teaching and instruction, particularly in the field of the Church's missionary activity,

(iv) ministries connected with the administration of the Church.

This list is not meant to be exhaustive. It indicates some of the areas where we believe that women and men are called to work together in the service of God's Kingdom, and where the many *charismata* of the Holy Spirit may function freely and fruitfully in the building up of the Church and society.

(3) But, while women exercise this diversity of ministries, it is not possible for them to be admitted to the priesthood. The ordination of women to the priesthood is an innovation, lacking any basis whatever in Holy Tradition. The Orthodox Church takes very seriously the admonition of St Paul, where the Apostle states with emphasis, repeating himself twice: 'But if we, or an angel from heaven, preaches to you anything else than what we have preached to you, let him be anathema. As we have already said, so I say to you now once more: if anyone preaches to you anything else than what you have received, let him be anathema' (Gal. 1.8–9).

From the time of Christ and the apostles onwards, the Church has ordained only men to the priesthood. Christians today are bound to remain faithful to the example of our Lord, to the testimony of Scripture, and to the constant and unvarying practice of the Church for two thousand years. In this constant and unvarying practice we see revealed the will of God and the testimony of the Holy Spirit, and we know that the Holy Spirit does not contradict himself.

(4) Holy Tradition is not static, but living and creative. Tradition is received by each succeeding generation in the same way, but in its own situation, and thus it is verified and enriched by the renewed experience that the People of God are continually gaining. On the basis of this renewed experience, the Spirit teaches us to be always responsive to the needs of the contemporary world. The Spirit does not bring us a new revelation, but enables us to

relive the truth revealed once for all in Jesus Christ, and continuously present in the Church. It is important, therefore, to distinguish between innovations and the creative continuity of Tradition. We Orthodox see the ordination of women not as part of this creative continuity, but as a violation of the apostolic faith and order of the Church.

(5) The action of ordaining women to the priesthood involves not simply a canonical point of Church discipline, but the basis of the Christian faith as expressed in the Church's ministries. If the Anglicans continue to ordain women to the priesthood, this will have a decisively negative effect on the issue of the recognition of Anglican Orders. Those Orthodox Churches which have partially or provisionally recognized Anglican Orders did so on the ground that the Anglican Church has preserved the apostolic succession; and the apostolic succession is not merely continuity in the outward laying on of hands, but signifies continuity in apostolic faith and spiritual life. By ordaining women, Anglicans would sever themselves from this continuity, and so any existing acts of recognition by the Orthodox would have to be reconsidered.

IV Anglican Positions on the Ordination of Women to the Priesthood

(1) The Anglican members of the Commission are unanimous in their desire to accept and maintain the tradition of the gospel, to which the prophets and apostles bear witness, and to be true to it in the life of the Church. They are divided over the ways in which that tradition should respond to the pressures of the world, over the extent to which the tradition may develop and change, and over the criteria by which to determine what developments within it are legitimate and appropriate. In the case of the ordination of women differences have become particularly acute and divisive within the Anglican Communion, now that the convictions of those in favour of it have been translated into action in certain national churches.

(2) On this question there is a diversity of views in the Anglican Communion and among the members of the Commission. There are those who believe that the ordination of women to the priesthood and the episcopate is in no way consonant with a true understanding of the Church's catholicity and apostolocity, but

rather constitutes a grave deformation of the Church's traditional faith and order. They therefore hope that under the guidance of the Holy Spirit, this practice will come to cease in our churches.

There are others who believe that the actions already taken constitute a proper extension and development of the Church's traditional ministry, and a necessary and prophetic response to the changing circumstances in which some churches are placed. They hope that in due time, under the guidance of the Spirit, these actions will be universally accepted.

There are others who regret the way in which the present action has been taken and believe that the time was not opportune nor the method appropriate for such action, although they see no absolute objection to it. Some of them hope that a way forward may be found which will allow for the distinct and complementary contributions of men and women to the Church's ordained ministry.

The minutes of the 1978 Athens Conference add the following presentation of Anglican views which were expressed at the time:

(1) Those Anglicans who in principle oppose the ordination of women do so for the reasons advanced by the Orthodox in this report. They would express their reasons as follows: the claim of the Anglican Communion to be catholic means that compelling reasons must be demonstrated for the rightness of such a break with catholic tradition. Those who oppose such a break believe that such reasons have not been forthcoming. On the contrary, they believe that there are fundamental reasons why such a break should not be made. These, in their judgement, come from a consideration of the Person of Christ. Although there is neither maleness nor femaleness in God, it was in a male that the Word was made flesh and humanity in all its fullness was united to the Godhead. They believe that this fact expresses the truth that the initiative in our redemption lies wholly with God, to whom the response of humanity must be creative obedience. For a woman to be the icon or sacramental expression of Christ as Head of the Church seems to them to be in opposition to the biblical images of the Church in relation to God, which consistently stress that humanity and the Church must be feminine in relation to God.

The New Testament indicates that the issue of headship and

authority, however qualified, cannot be divorced either from the created relationship between man and woman, for instance in marriage, or from the instituted relationship between the ordained ministry and the congregation. They believe that a male priest must be the symbol and image of Christ as Bridegroom, whereas women, supremely exemplified in Mary, to whom was given the highest vocation of any created being, must be the symbol and image of the response of humanity in creative obedience. They believe that the God-given nature of the ministerial priesthood includes the fact that it is male. A refusal to accept this fact leads in their judgement, not only to a distortion of man's understanding of his relationship to God, but also to a distortion of his understanding of the redemption of the deepest aspects of his humanity. Finally, the opponents believe that the ordination of women to the priesthood is divisive because it is wrong, rather than wrong because it is divisive.

(2) Those members of the Commission who advocate the ordination of women to the priesthood now, do so because they believe that the Church's tradition must grow and develop if the Church is to remain faithful to its mission to the world. More particularly, they believe that this is a true development, under the guidance of the Holy Spirit, of the patterns of ministry to which God has been calling some Churches in response to major changes in the ordering of society. The vocations of women who offer themselves for the priestly ministry require therefore to be tested, and none of the arguments, either from Scripture or tradition, advanced against such vocations seem to those who hold this position to be in principle convincing. In particular they hold that arguments which suggest that priests must be male in order either to represent the maleness of God, a position held by no one in this Commission, or because the maleness of Christ is of soteriological significance, are based on serious doctrinal errors. Since priesthood represents humanity to God and God to humanity, it is humanity and not maleness which is the decisive qualification for exercising priesthood, just as in Christ, according to catholic doctrine, it is his humanity which is of soteriological significance and not the accidents of his humanity. Further they argue that to insist on an all-male priesthood in societies which have abandoned all-male leadership in other areas of life is

in effect to distort the meaning of Christian priesthood. This may lead to serious distortions in doctrine. Thirdly, they believe that the ordination of women would lead to an enrichment of the Christian priesthood by bringing to it women's gifts and wisdom, as well as by deepening the Christian understanding of the divine saving initiative in Jesus Christ which is represented by the priesthood.

(3) There are other members of the Commission who, while they find these theological arguments valid and convincing, yet believe for reasons of an ecclesiological nature that action in this matter should not be taken precipitately.

APPENDIX 3

Anglican–Orthodox Joint Doctrinal Commission

ANGLICAN PARTICIPANTS 1984

The Revd Canon A. M. Allchin   *Church of England*
The Revd Roger Beckwith   *Church of England*
The Revd Colin Davey (Secretary)   *Church of England*
The Revd Professor Eugene Fairweather   *Anglican Church of Canada*
The Revd Dr John Gaden   *Anglican Church of Australia*
Mr Kiranga Gatimu   *Church of the Province of Kenya*
The Revd Professor W. B. Green   *The Episcopal Church in the USA*
The Rt Revd Richard Hanson   *Church of England*
The Rt Revd Henry Hill (Co-Chairman)   *Anglican Church of Canada*
The Revd Canon John McNab   *Church of the Province of the West Indies*
The Revd Dr William A. Norgren   *The Episcopal Church in the USA*
The Revd Professor Oliver O'Donovan   *Church of England*
The Revd John Riches   *The Episcopal Church of Scotland*
The Rt Revd Richard Rutt   *Church of England*
The Revd Dr John M. Sentamu   *Church of Uganda*
The Rt Revd Dr Maxwell Thomas   *Anglican Church of Australia*
The Revd Canon Hugh Wybrew   *Church of England*

Not Present at 1984 meeting

The Rt Revd Samir Kafity   *Episcopal Church in Jerusalem and the Middle East*
The Revd Luke Pato   *Church of the Province of Southern Africa*
The Rt Revd Robert E. Terwilliger   *The Episcopal Church in the USA*

Other Anglican Participants 1977–83

The Right Revd R. A. K. Runcie 1977–8 (Co-Chairman)   *Church of England*
The Revd Canon M. J. D. Carmichael 1977–81   *The Church of the Province of South Africa*
The Rt Revd V. Cornish 1981   *Anglican Church of Australia*
The Revd Canon Edward Every 1977–80   *The Episcopal Church of Jerusalem and the Middle East*
The Revd Dr Edward Hardy 1977–80   *The Episcopal Church in the USA*
The Rt Revd Mark Santer 1977–82   *Church of England*
The Rt Revd Graham Leonard 1977–80   *Church of England*

The Revd Dr John Mbiti 1980–1   *Church of the Province of Kenya*
The Rt Revd Graham Delbridge 1977–8   *Anglican Church of Australia*
The Revd Dr Richard Norris 1977   *The Episcopal Church in the USA*
The Rt Revd Jonathan Sherman 1977   *The Episcopal Church in the USA*

Consultants
Dr Paul Anderson 1977   *The Episcopal Church in the USA*
The Revd John de Satgé 1977   *Church of England*

ORTHODOX PARTICIPANTS 1984
Ecumenical Patriarchate
The Most Revd Archbishop Methodios of Thyateira and Great Britain
(Co-Chairman)
The Rt Revd Bishop Aristarchos of Zenoupolis

Patriarchate of Antioch
The Rt Revd Bishop Gabriel

Patriarchate of Jerusalem
The Most Revd Metropolitan Basil of Caesarea
Professor George Galitis

Patriarchate of Moscow
The Most Revd Archbishop Basil of Brussels and All Belgium
The Very Revd Professor Livery Voronov

Patriarchate of Romania
The Very Revd Archimandrite Nifon Mihaita

Patriarchate of Bulgaria
The Very Revd Professor Nikolay Chivarov

Church of Cyprus
The Most Revd Metropolitan Chrysostomos of Kition

Church of Greece
Professor Constantine Scouteris

Church of Poland
Mr Nikolaj Kozlowski

Church of Finland
Hieromonk Ambrosius

Orthodox Consultant
The Rt Revd Bishop Kallistos of Diocleia

Orthodox Secretariat
The Very Revd Dr George Dragas   (Secretary)
Dr Andreas Tillyrides
The Very Revd Archimandrite Athanasios Theocharous

Not present at 1984 meeting

Patriarchate of Alexandria
The Most Revd Metropolitan Petros of Aksum

Patriarchate of Antioch
The Very Revd Archimandrite Gregory Saliby

Patriarchate of Serbia
Professor Stojan Gosevic

Patriarchate of Romania
Professor Nikolai Chitescu

Church of Greece
The Very Revd Professor John Romanides

Church of Finland
The Most Revd Metropolitan John of Helsinki

Other Orthodox Participants 1977–83

Ecumenical Patriarchate
The Most Revd Archbishop Athenagoras of Thyateira and Great Britain
1977–8   (Co-Chairman)
The Most Revd Archbishop Stylianos, Archbishop of Australia 1977–8
The Rt Revd Gregory of Tropaeou 1977–8

Patriarchate of Alexandria
The Most Revd Metropolitan Dionysios of Memphis 1981–2

Patriarchate of Moscow
The Most Revd Archbishop Vladimir of Dmitrov 1982

Patriarchate of Serbia
The Very Revd Professor G. Gardashevich 1981

Patriarchate of Romania
Mr Nicolae Mihaitza 1977
Deacon Dr Petru Y. David 1978
The Revd Silviu-Petre Pufulete 1980–1

Orthodox Consultant
Mr Nicholas Lossky 1977

Orthodox Secretariat
The Very Revd Archimandrite Meletios 1977
The Rt Revd Bishop Timothy of Melitoupolis 1980–2
The Very Revd Archimandrite Symeon Lash 1982–3

APPENDIX 4

List of Papers by Members of the Commission

AOJDD *Title, author and details of publication*

Meeting in Oxford 1973

37B   Comprehensiveness and the Mission of the Church
      The Revd A. M. Allchin
      Published in *Theology*, vol. lxxv, no. 630 (Dec. 1972) and in
      The Kingdom of Love and Knowledge (Darton, Longman &
      Todd 1979).

43   The Thirty-Nine Articles
      The Revd A. M. Allchin
      Published in *Theology*, vol. lxxv, no. 630 (Dec. 1972).

52   Answers by Anglican delegates to questions put to them by mem-
      bers of the Orthodox Commission
      Published with AOJDD 43 in *Theology*, vol. lxxv, no. 630 (Dec.
      1972).

66   The Holy Spirit as Interpreter of the Gospel and Giver of Life in
      the Church today
      Metropolitan Stylianos of Miletoupolos.

67   The Atonement of Christ on the Cross and in the Resurrection
      Archbishop Basil of Brussels and All Belgium.

Meeting in Crete 1974

78   Inspiration and Revelation in the Holy Scriptures
      Part I by the Revd R. Beckwith
      Part II by the Revd C. Davey.

80   Inspiration and Revelation in the Holy Scriptures
      Professor N. Chitescu.
      Published in *Mitropolia Olteniei*, Craiova-Romania, 1-3 (1978),
      pp. 27-41.

84   Revelation and Divine Inspiration in the Holy Scriptures
      Professor George Galitis.

Meeting in Romania 1974

74   The *Filioque*
      Canon E. Every.

76   The Councils, Icons and Christology
      Canon E. Every.

77   Anglicans and the Decisions of the Seventh Ecumenical Council
      Canon A. M. Allchin.

82   The Authority of the Ecumenical Synods
      Metropolitan John of Helsinki.

Meeting in London 1975

Meeting in Cambridge 1977

I

193A   Man, Woman and the Priesthood of Christ.
        Archimandrite Kallistos Ware. Published in P. Moore (ed.), *Man, Woman and Priesthood* (London 1978), pp. 68–90.

193B   Facing the Problem of the Ordination of Women to the Priesthood.
        Metropolitan Methodius of Aksum.
        Published in *Ekklesiastikos Pharos*, vol. 61 (1979), pp. 247–56.

Meeting in Llandaff 1980

I

207   Church and Eucharist, Communion and Intercommunion.
        Archimandrite Kallistos Ware.
        Published in *Sobornost*, 7:7 (1978), pp. 550–67; reissued separately by Light and Life Publishing Company (Minneapolis 1980).

210   The Church and the Churches
        Bishop R. P. C. Hanson.

211   General Introduction to 'The Church and Churches'
        Professor N. Chitescu.

II

212   The Communion of Saints
212A   The Communion of Saints in recent Welsh Poetry
212B   The Prayers of the Saints
        All 212 by Canon A. M. Allchin.

216   Death and the Communion of Saints: Notes on Orthodox Teaching and Practice
        Archimandrite Kallistos Ware
        Published in *Sobornost*, incorporating *Eastern Churches Review*, 3:2 (1981), pp. 179–91.

III

213   The *Filioque* Clause in Ecumenical Perspective: a preliminary Anglican Response
        The Revd Professor E. Fairweather

214   The *Filioque* in Ecumenical Perspective
214A   Supplementary to the *Filioque* Paper
        All 214 by Archbishop Methodios of Thyateira and Great Britain.

215   A Statement by Archbishop Methodios of Thyateira and Great Britain.

Meeting in Chambésy 1981

I

231   Anglican Understanding of the Church
        The Revd C. Davey.

Meeting in Odessa 1983

I

II

III